YOU'RE ~~NOT~~ FIRED

AS A RESULT OF MERGERS, ACQUISITIONS & REORGANIZATIONS

D. N. S.

authorHOUSE®

AuthorHouse™
1663 Liberty Drive
Bloomington, IN 47403
www.authorhouse.com
Phone: 1 (800) 839-8640

Published by AuthorHouse 07/22/2015

ISBN: 978-1-4259-4056-0 (sc)
ISBN: 978-1-4259-2513-0 (e)

To my wife, who has been my partner during the mergers, acquisitions, and reorganizations I've gone through during my professional career.

Table of Contents

Preface

Mergers, acquisitions, and reorganizations (MARo) have occurred since the Industrial Revolution. During the late seventies and early eighties, however, the seeds of globalization were sown. The seeds began to bloom, accelerating the MARo activities and impacting millions of professionals like you. Two of the by-products of globalization were mergers/acquisitions between companies and reorganizations within companies. Many professionals were demoted, shifted, or laid off, while a few were promoted. Reorganizations in a company may occur without a merger or an acquisition. It may be a way for the company to make processes more efficient, reduce redundancies, and ultimately make the company more profitable. Reorganizations may mean that groups are combined or sometimes split.

This condensed and focused book examines the merger, acquisition, integration, and resultant reorganization process; it identifies potential pitfalls in handling changes, and it recommends ways for you to protect and promote yourself before, during, and after the changes. Worksheets for checking how you are doing before, during, and after the merger, acquisition, or reorganization are provided. The readers are encouraged to use the worksheets to measure themselves and continually adjust in order to come out ahead. The end of the book contains a bonus chapter providing a checklist for successful career planning. The book concludes with a multitude of valuable references in the area of career building.

The author has over twenty-five years of firsthand experience with MARo as a bench worker, supervisor, and a manager. During his career, he has constantly moved up in spite of several mergers, acquisitions, and reorganizations by employing the secrets provided in this book. It is author's earnest hope that the reader will take advantage of these practical and value-added teachings for his or her benefit regardless of the profession.

The author expresses special thanks to all provided valuable critique, editing, and recommendations for the book.

Anatomy of Mergers, Acquisitions, and Reorganizations (MARo)

Mergers, acquisitions, and reorganizations are like building a plane while it is in flight. This brings unique challenges to all involved in the process. During mergers and acquisitions (M&A), companies want their businesses to move forward without interruptions or delays. For that, they need their key associates in place. Companies of all sizes merge, acquire, and reorganize for a variety of reasons—one of the most common reasons being economics. Other reasons behind mergers and acquisitions are lack of critical mass, lack of new research products, market share shrinking, market globalization, and so forth.

Whatever the reason behind the change, one of the main goals of the merger or acquisition process is to integrate the companies involved as efficiently and as quickly as possible. This process invariably affects the size of the merged or acquired companies, which typically translates into downsizing (some companies call it "rightsizing") and layoffs. The process of MARo may take anywhere from weeks to several months. During this period, one should take the necessary steps so that he or she is not caught in the downsizing before, during, or after the changes take place.

When companies of approximately the same size combine, it is called a merger, and both sides are affected. For example, management for the new company may come from both sides; if divisions or sites are downsized or closed, usually the same numbers on both sides are affected. The reduction in force may occur equally between the merged companies, and a number of positions are filled from both sides.

When one company acquires another (typically a larger one acquires a smaller one; however, it could happen the other way around), the impact on the smaller partner may be greater, especially in the management area. If the acquisition is an "unfriendly" one, expect an immediate removal of the management team from the acquired company. Often, the so-called merger of equals may not be equal in practice, and one company may take the lead and eventually run the combined company. Be cognizant of this possibility, and prepare yourself to tilt toward the major merging partner.

If mergers and acquisitions are like building a plane while it is flying, then reorganizations are like fixing a plane while it is flying. Usually, reorganizations precede mergers and acquisitions. Both future partners try to make their respective organizations "look alike" prior to the change so that, after the change, the combined company runs as smoothly as possible. Reorganization may also occur after mergers and acquisitions in order to optimize the combined company. Sometimes, reorganizations are done to fix things that aren't broken, while other things that need fixing are ignored, resulting in major problems.

Mergers and acquisitions bring uncertainties and make the organizations unsettled, resulting in a lot of frustrations among associates. Mergers and acquisitions also bring cultural and ego clashes. The "lay of the land" may change drastically as a result of these activities, and you should position yourself to fit into the "new land." The trick during this period is to keep doing what you are doing while keeping your ears close to the ground. Be sure to listen to any changes that may affect you so that you can avert any negative impact. Remember, merging and acquiring companies want greatly to keep their businesses going and growing during and after the change. Upper management is keen to identify and keep key associates who are top performers and produce results. You want to become one who produces results.

Intercompany reorganizations occur as needed, regardless of the type of business you are in or the size of the company. Reorganizations are often done to reduce or eliminate redundancies and unnecessary headcounts, increase efficiencies, and ultimately improve profitability. Companies often reorganize in response to the changing marketplace, customer expectations, regulatory environment, and so forth. You, as an employee, should stay on top of the reorganization process by creating a network within your company. Sometimes, you may find out about the reorganization from some other department rather than from your own. Use the knowledge gained from your network to position yourself and maximize your growth in the company.

Often, completion of M&A takes an extended period of time for a variety of reasons. It could take anywhere from twelve to twenty-four months. A few M&As are done very quickly by design. Reacting to fast mergers or acquisitions becomes a challenge to employees. Preplanning and organization on your part will help you to come out on top.

Mergers, acquisitions, and reorganizations can be divided into three distinct phases in terms of activities, impact on individuals, and impact on the overall company. Phase 1 entails the pre-MARo activities, and it is usually benign to most associates, especially those who are not in the upper management. Rumors typically begin in this phase, and it is important to stay tuned to the rumors, as they often provide valuable telltale signs. Phase 2 of the change is the most important phase; it is when a lot of MARo-related activities occur, and these could have a significant impact on you and your career. This phase encompasses the activities that set the tone of the new organization. This phase could be divided into Phase 2a and Phase 2b for convenience and to aid in understanding the activities and maturation of the whole MARo process. Usually, in Phase 2a, the combining companies identify key people, processes, and projects/products that need to be immediately combined and streamlined. In this phase, particularly, the combined companies want to make sure that the plane is still flying while it is being built, meaning that the ongoing business (research and development, manufacturing, sales and marketing, etc.) is still moving ahead. In Phase 2b, the integration teams are formed, and the activities progress in combining people, processes, projects, and projects/products. During the overall Phase 2, people leave the company on their own for a variety of reasons and sometimes are asked to leave. Many who leave the company do so because they feel threatened or feel that their abilities are not being appreciated. People leaving the company creates chaos, uncertainties, disorders, and, for some, new opportunities. Typically, in Phase 2b, new opportunities become evident, and you may want to take advantage of them. The last phase of MARos, Phase 3, is characterized by the activities after the merger is "over." It should be noted that a merger or an acquisition is not over on a given day or month; it continues for a considerable period of time after it is "over."

Mergers and acquisitions bring about a sustained period of constraints, especially in the area of available staffing. The trick in surviving a MARo is to really know the people, processes, and projects/products of your company, as well as those of the other company that is being merged or acquired. MARos are stressful to organizations and associates. Differences in cultures between the combining companies should be taken as an asset instead of a negative. Associates who really understand the cultural differences and adapt to the differences move ahead. Cultural differences, such as centralized decisions versus team-based decisions, often bother associates in a merged company. Associates who were used to team-based decisions prior to merger get frustrated with a centralized decision process in the merged company. In this case, one must learn to adapt and carry out the decisions made at the center of the company.

The Telltale Signs of MARo

MARos invariably involve people, processes, and projects/products. There are several common telltale signs of an impending MARo. The first and foremost sign includes rumors that start and circulate from higher levels within the company. Rumors of a merger or acquisition are akin to the saying that where there is smoke, there is fire. Sometimes, the upper management may "leak out" information as a rumor just to scare off associates and in the hope that the weaker ones will leave the company. Rumors may subside for a period of time; however, they reappear and become persistent. And that should give a clue that MARo is imminent.

The second sign of an impending MARo is when a hiring freeze is imposed in spite of financial well-being, often without warning. Prior to a merger, participating companies often try to match respective functions and departments and figure out redundancies. The management of both merging companies often tries to reduce the headcount prior to the merger so that redundancies after the merger are reduced or preferably eliminated.

The third sign of an impending MARo is that companies cut unnecessary expenses by cutting travel. Most travel expenses are nice to have but are not essential. Hence, prior to a merger (those which are friendly), companies will reduce nonessential travel expenses. During this period of travel cost reductions, companies will manage to do their business by teleconferences instead of traveling. When MARos are friendly and expected, often mid- and senior-level managers are promoted for apparent no reason to the associates in the merging companies. These promotions occur in order to match management layers of both companies as closely as possible. Prior to a MARo activity, various sites are often closed or sold. Obviously, the main reason for the closing or selling of sites is to improve efficiencies and financials after the MARo activity is implemented. After instituting a hiring freeze, companies find out that they may still have to reduce the headcount—a fixed expense—after the merger and announce a reduction in force. This becomes a very good sign of upcoming MARo activity.

Another sign of MARo is when some senior management people leave the company without any apparent reason. This happens because the senior management learns of the impending MARo activity and recognizes that they may not have a spot in the newly merged organization, and they decide to leave the company. When two companies merge, they may end up with similar products that may not be acceptable to the Federal Trade Commission (FTC) or similar government agency. The FTC often objects to one single type of product being sold by one company and asks the merged company to sell their products that are similar.

Another telltale sign of MARo for a publicly traded company is when the stock price of merging companies goes up for no apparent reason. Sometimes, when a company fails to introduce new products in the marketplace for a long time or its research-and-development pipeline dries up, it becomes a target of acquisition. This could become a telltale sign of an upcoming MARo activity.

It should be noted that any one of the above telltale signs could occur in a company that is not potentially being merged or acquired. However, a combination of the above signs could become a high-probability signal of upcoming MARo-related changes.

In the next chapter, let's examine the first phase of MARo activity, which is what one should do prior to the change.

Phase 1 (Pre-MARo):
What You Should Do Prior to the Change

As soon as you notice one or more of the telltale signs of M&A, you should immediately evaluate your own personal situation in light of the potential change. First and foremost, you should assess your strengths and weaknesses based on the most recent activities you performed or your most recent job performance evaluation. This type of assessment will give you an honest picture of you and help you to decide where you may fit in the new organization. It is important that, in the new organization, you land in the most optimal position, which will allow you to grow. The second thing you should do is ask your immediate supervisor to give you a written job evaluation. If you disagree with the job evaluation done by your supervisor, do not hesitate to raise the issue with the next level up in management, as well with the human resources department. The job evaluation done prior to MARo is often used in the integration process and in the creation of new departments. Besides securing a job performance evaluation from your immediate supervisor prior to the MARo, you should also try to get a job performance evaluation from other senior-level management. Until MARo activity is over, insist on regular quarterly job performance evaluations. Remember—there is a possibility that, after the MARo activity, your immediate supervisor may not be there to give you a job evaluation! Next, based on the above analysis, identify a developmental plan to address your weaknesses. If you can take care of the developmental plan prior to MARo, it will benefit you tremendously after the MARo. Once you know which company might merge with your company, find out from your internal as well as external network about the people, R&D projects, and commercially available products of the other company. Knowledge of the products of the other company gives you a leg up during the integration process in Phase 2 and other activities in Phase 3 of MARo. As part of the upcoming merger activity, if reorganization within your company is being planned, stay tuned with the plans. However, do not actively participate in it until the dust settles. What you might see in the initial stage of the reorganization may not turn out to be final. Apply a "wait-and-see" philosophy at this stage. Even though it is always advisable to form a network with at least two levels of the management, it is critical to do so at this phase of MARo, as it will pay off at the later stage. When the newly merged company selects associates at all levels, earlier networking will help you to survive or even move ahead. Companies often offer new assignments or promotions to some of their associates prior to MARo activity. One should carefully investigate and analyze these types of assignments and promotions and decide whether or not to accept them. Sometimes, promotions or new assignments right before MARo are given to get rid of certain positions or associates. As soon as you know that the merger or acquisition may be imminent, increase your visibility by giving presentations at outside professional conferences; someone from the other company may be present at the meeting and will recognize you during and after the M&A, and it will bring name recognition in the next two critical phases of MARo.

In the next phase of MARo, companies form integration teams for all parts of the business. Try to get into the integration teams when they are formed. Make recommendations to your management on how things could be different in your department; this signals that you have the necessary leadership qualities to participate in the integration process with the other company—which may have different ways of doing things. Identify a couple of mentors within the company who could assist you during and after the M&A change. Focus on "the three Ps" of your company—study your company's people, processes, and projects/products very well. This knowledge will prove to be quite useful during and after the merger and especially during the integration process. Keep your resume updated in this phase, since you never know when you may need it. (Actually, it is a good idea to update your resume at least once a year). Also, sharpen your network inside (other related departments) and outside the company (recruiters, friends in other companies, etc.). Last but not least, you should be careful about your own compensation aspects within the current company. After MARos, companies often combine or eliminate various compensation packages (bonuses, 401(k), stock options, health savings plans, etc.), and you should be very careful and make sure that your total financial package does not get changed in the shuffle of the books during MARo activity. For example, after the MARo activity is completed, your stocks in the former company may be recalculated for the newly merged company, and you want to make sure that errors do not occur. You should print out all of the balances in your various accounts with the company and keep a weekly tally of various packages.

Phase 2: What You Should Do During the MARo Change

This is the most important phase of any MARo, and it could have a big impact on your future at the company. Assume for the moment that your company has announced a merger or an acquisition with another company, and the wheels are turning to blend the companies, reduce expenses, and blend cultures. Transition and integration teams are also being formed. The following steps are recommended during this important phase of combining companies. In this early phase (2a) of M&A, typically senior-level managers are involved. Keep an eye on the changes to see who stays in power and who does not, since it could be the foundation upon which the rest of the new organization will be built.

Invariably, one of the themes during this phase of M&A that comes out is "We are right; we know how to do things correctly. They (the other company) are wrong, and they don't know how to do things correctly." Don't get caught up in this "us-and-they" mentality. People find out that, in most cases, it is just a different way of doing business, and there is no absolute right or wrong way of doing things. People who show the flexibility and accept the "other way" and provide solutions usually move up in the new organization. Accept (instead of fighting to not accept) the decisions made at this stage of the change; typically, decisions made at this stage are not final. Most likely, the players will change.

The integration teams are formed based on the experience of associates, their special skills, and flexibility shown in the past. The integration teams, which are typically made up of an equal number of associates from both sides of the merging companies, share (a) organizational structures, (b) their way of conducting business, (c) strengths and weaknesses of their current systems, (d) desire to get the best practices of the emerging companies, and so forth. Companies and associates who set aside their egos and take the best practices out of both companies usually succeed in the new company. Be a team player. During the integration team meetings, don't shy away from suggesting new or better ways of doing things based on your experience. Make every attempt to speak up at the integration meetings. Update your management (at least two levels) on the progress of the integration team and your individual inputs. During the merger, continue to document your performance evaluations with your human resources department. This is very important for your future in the newly combined company. During the M&A activities, if you notice that there may be a possibility for you or your department to relocate, consider it seriously. It is human nature not to accept a move or change, but in the long run, the move may turn out to be beneficial. Accepting a move also shows your management that you are flexible and open to change. During M&A activities, openings may come up with other departments, and if you happen to have relevant expertise, consider taking that option. Sometimes, M&A activities include disposing of associates whom the management does not like. Be aware of these situations and take steps to protect yourself. Find a mentor within the organization who could protect you if something like that occurs. Refrain from saying negative things about your current company or supervisor/management. This will leave a bad impression on the new company management. Companies often hire consultants to assist with the merger process. Get to know the consultants—their backgrounds, other companies for whom they have consulted, and their philosophies. Members of a consulting company usually interview several key associates from both companies in order to understand the processes, strengths, and weaknesses of the organizations. The consultant may not know the details of your business, but they know processes that will work for your company. Make every effort to participate with the consultants and try to influence the process. You may experience frustrations during the merger process mainly due to the company feels somewhat unsettled. Cope with the frustrations. Once the company settles down, you will find clarity. Again, pay close attention to "the three developing Ps" of the upcoming combined company—people, processes, and projects/products. The more you understand about "the three Ps," the more it will help you after the merger. Finally, as you did during Phase 1 of MARo activity, pay special attention to your financials in the company. Employees often ignore this one aspect or do not take care of it in a timely manner during MARo activity. As mentioned earlier, during and especially after MARo activity, some or all parts of your compensation may be affected and changed. Again, review and document all parts of your compensation package.

Phase 3: What You Should Do After the MARo Is Over

Now the merger or the acquisition is over, and one new company has been formed. This phase of a merger or acquisition activity is of secondary importance after the previous phases of activities during the merger and acquisition. Often, within three to six months after the completion of a merger and acquisition, senior people from the new company leave, resulting in a ripple effect in the organization that may affect you. In other words, the organization remains quite fluid. In this phase, integration teams' work may be reevaluated, and the outcome from previous phases may be modified. Post-M&A fine-tuning often occurs in the organization and processes. Take an active role during the fine-tuning process by making suggestions and appropriate contributions. This will help your career in the future within the new company. As a result of M&A, job functions often change, and you may move into a new group or be promoted within the same job function. If you have moved into a new job or if you have moved up, you should quickly learn the new job and establish your leadership role within the new company. This is quite important, because the management in the new company will carefully evaluate the impact of the change on the organization. Quickly learn "the three Ps" (people, processes, and projects/products) of the other company. A lack of knowledge often exists about the newly combined company following a merger and acquisition, because people have either moved around or left the company. This lack of knowledge creates a vacuum, and you should be ready to fill up the vacuum. Your know-how of the newly combined company will again assist you in protecting yourself and may even assist you in moving up in your career. M&A activities typically result in overcapacity, and sites may have to be closed (rationalized). A combined company will try to improve its balance sheet by closing sites. If sites are closed or rationalized, actively participate in the decision process and the moving of products in an efficient and timely manner. When sites are closed, products are moved to the receiving site, and a lot of work needs to be done in order to facilitate the transfer. The newly merged company will need experts during site rationalization so that the transfers are done with a minimal negative impact on the supply chain and inventory. In this phase of MARo, align yourself with the power players of the newly combined company. This suggestion could be true for any phase of MARo; however, it should be noted that the power players at earlier stages may not be there when the new company is formed. Making connections and networking with power players later on may be too late and may not have a positive impact on your career. Actively participate in speaking within the company so that the new members who came from the other company come to know you quickly and appreciate your role. You want to show your expertise and strengths to the new members of the merged company so that you get a proper role and the opportunity to grow. If you have new management as a result of the MARo, employ and utilize all of those quarterly and annual job performance reviews you had prior to and during the merger with the new management. Remember that the new management most likely does not know you from a performance perspective, and it is your job to educate them about you. Your future career with the newly combined company depends, in part, on your networking within the new company. For the reasons stated earlier, most jobs in a newly merged company often are roughly equivalent to making a job change and going to a different company.

After the M&A, the new company will have its own characteristics, culture, and way of doing things. Understand them and apply them to your daily work. One of the examples of culture changes in the new company may be a centralized versus a decentralized decision process. Associates from a company where decisions were made by teams and approved by the senior management may get frustrated to find in the new company that the decisions are made by the senior management without the input from individuals or teams. With these types of changes, one must go with the flow and be flexible. At the end of the M&A, the new company will establish Standard Operating Procedures (SOPs) or Work Practices (WPs). These SOPs and WPs are like glue in the combined new company, which now has new people, new processes, and new projects/products. Make yourself available in the development of SOPs and WPs, and influence the way in which they are developed. Last but not least, check your total compensation package and its components (401(k), health savings account, etc.) to make sure that it is not adversely affected due to some inadvertent error at the end of MARo activity. At the beginning of the newly merged company, tally all of the balances from your previous company with that with the new company.

Summary: Steps to Protect Your Career During MARo

1. When you join a company, develop a plan to network within the company as well as outside of the company. This networking will help you during and after the MARo.

2. Develop some very good personal business practices and habits—come on time to work, plan your day the day before, go to meetings on time, go prepared, participate in meetings, follow-up on your commitments, and provide results.

3. Understand the mechanics of M&A. The business needs to go forward while the process of consolidation is going on, and that is a tricky thing to do. Prepare yourself so that you become a valuable employee who participates in building the newly combined company while keeping the business going.

4. Use your influence and connections to get into the integration teams between merging companies. The integration teams usually play a critical role in the new company.

5. Participate fully in the transition teams that are formed during the M&A process. The integration teams are usually the seeds of the future new company.

6. Study the integration teams' objectives, purpose, and the end product. Plan backward from the end product to the current situation; it will help you participate in team meetings. Don't be afraid to make suggestions. Keep your visibility up within and outside the integration teams.

7. In the integration team meetings, focus on the positive of the companies and keep the mentality of "us-and-they" away. Mergers and acquisitions often fail because the majority of the people involved suffer from the "us-and-they" syndrome, and senior managers are aware of this.

8. As soon as you confirm M&A, get your performance evaluation done by three other associates (sometimes called a "360-degree evaluation") besides your immediate supervisor. Collect all evaluations, keep copies of all of them, and submit them to your human resources department.

9. Once you know the merging company, study "the three Ps" (people, processes, and projects/products) of the other company and employ the knowledge during the transition to your advantage.

10. During the integration team meetings, take a leadership or coleadership role.

11. Explore other opportunities in the newly combined company, and if they are available, consider those that could result in promotion.

12. As a result of a merger, if the company asks you to move to another city or location, accept it as an opportunity.

13. Be a team player during and after the M&A process. In an environment of "unknown" and "unsettled," the company needs people who can work in a team.

14. Become a solution provider instead of a problem identifier in the company. Take every problem as an opportunity to provide a solution. The management especially likes and appreciates associates who not only identify problems but who also provide solutions to issues and problems.

Your Convenient Worksheet to Measure How You Are Doing In the Midst of a Potential MARo

The following pages give you a vehicle to document how you are doing prior to, during, and after each phase of a MARo. This should allow you to adjust your strategies accordingly for surviving and even advancing.

Worksheets For Telltale Signs of a MARo

Based on chapter 1, document (including dates)
any of the telltale signs that you see.

Activity	Date of Assessment	Comments (Including Follow-Ups)
1. Rumors start and circulate from higher levels.		
2. A hiring freeze is imposed in spite of financial well-being, often without warning.		
3. Travelling expenses are cut drastically.		
4. Reorganization—including company-wide senior level promotions—occurs.		
5. Sites are reduced or sold.		

Activity	Date of Assessment	Comments (Including Follow-Ups)
6. There is a reduction in force.		
7. Some senior management people have left the company for no apparent reason.		
8. Products are sold that are apparently doing well.		
9. The stock price of the company shot up for no apparent reason.		
10. The R&D pipeline has dried up, and/or the market share has dropped.		

Whenever possible, confirm and reconfirm any or all of the above telltale signs and document them in the above table. This will assist you in planning ahead of MARo if it does occur. If and when the telltale signs turn out to be true and a MARo occurs, follow the next two series of worksheets.

Worksheets For What You Should Do
Prior to a MARo (Phase 1)

After seeing the telltale signs of MARo, prepare
yourself for Phase 1 of MARo.

Activity	Response	Date(s)	Comments
1. Assess your strengths and weaknesses.			
2. Insist on quarterly job performance evaluations.			
3. Identify a developmental plan to address your weaknesses.			

Activity	Response	Date(s)	Comments
4. Use your internal as well as external network (who is who in the other company) and learn about "the three Ps" (people, processes, and projects/products) of the other company.			
5. If some sort of reorganization is being planned, stay tuned. However, do not actively participate at this stage.			
6. Form a network with the next two levels above you within your company.			
7. In case of a new offer or an assignment, carefully analyze it and then act.			

Activity	Response	Date(s)	Comments
8. Increase your visibility by giving presentations outside at professional meetings.			
9. Keep your eyes and ears open to any movement within your organization, which may signal the pending merger or acquisition.			
10. Make recommendations to your management as to how things could be different in your department, thereby sending signals that you have the necessary leadership qualities to participate in the integration process.			

Activity	Response	Date(s)	Comments
11. Identify a couple of mentors within the company who could assist you during and after M&A.			
12. Focus on "the three Ps" of your company. Study your company's people, processes, and projects/products.			
13. Focus on your various financial packages (e.g., 401(k), health savings account, etc.) within your company.			

At the end of this phase, you have learned that the M&A has gone through, and you are getting into the most important phase, which could have a significant impact on your future career.

Worksheet For What You Should Do
During the M&A (Phase 2)

Now that you know that the M&A has been announced, you should focus on this pivotal and critical phase of the process. Based on chapter 3, you should document below the details regarding how you are progressing.

Activity	Response	Date	Comments
1. Keep an eye on the changes to see who from the senior management stays in power and who does not. Use this knowledge to assess the situation.			
2. Show flexibility by accepting the other company's ideas. (Don't get caught into the "us-and-they" mentality.)			

Activity	Response	Date	Comments
3. Accept (instead of fighting to not accept) the decisions made at this stage of the change, since typically decisions made at this stage are not final.			
4. The integration teams are formed based on the experience of associates, their special skills, and flexibility shown in the past. Share your special skills and flexibility with your management.			
5. Companies and associates who set aside their egos and take the best practices out of both companies usually succeed in the new company. Be a team player.			

Activity	Response	Date	Comments
6. During the integration team meetings, don't shy away from suggesting new or better ways of doing things based on your experience. Make every attempt to speak up at the integration meetings.			
7. Update your management (on at least two levels) on the progress of the integration team and your individual input.			
8. Accept if the company asks you to move as a result of MARo. This will show to your management that you are flexible and open to change.			

Activity	Response	Date	Comments
9. During M&A activities, openings may come up with other departments, and if you happen to have relevant expertise, con-sider taking those options.			
10. Sometimes, M&A activities dis-pose of associates whom the manage-ment does not like. Be aware of these situations and take steps to protect yourself. Find a mentor within the organization who could protect you if something like that occurs.			

Activity	Response	Date	Comments
11. Refrain from saying negative things about your current company or supervisor/management. This will leave a bad impression on the new company management.			
12. Make every effort to participate with the consultants (if the company brings them in), and try to influence the process.			
13. You may experience frustrations during the merger process mainly due to the company feels somewhat unsettled. Cope with the frustrations. List your frustrations, and get help to address them.			

Activity	Response	Date	Comments
14. Again, pay close attention to "the three Ps" of the upcoming, newly combined company—people, processes, and projects/ products.			
15. Pay attention to your financial packages at the company. List all of the current amounts/ holdings in each of the packages.			

Worksheets For What You Should Do
After the MARo Is Over (Phase 3)

Now the M&A is over, and one of the companies has been formed. You should be looking at the future in the newly combined company. Based on chapter 5, you should document your progress in the following worksheet.

Activities	Response	Date	Comments
1. Take an active role during this phase of MARo (fine-tuning process) by making suggestions and appropriate contributions.			
2. As a result of the M&A, if you have moved into a new job or have moved up, you should quickly learn the new job and establish your leadership.			

Activities	Response	Date	Comments
3. Quickly learn more about "the three Ps" (people, processes, and projects/products) of the other company.			
4. As a result of M&A activities, if sites are closed or rationalized, actively participate in moving products in an efficient manner.			
5. Align yourself with the power players of the newly combined company.			

Activities	Response	Date	Comments
6. Post M&A, actively participate in giving talks within the company so that the new members who came from the other company come to know you quickly and appreciate your role.			
7. Employ and utilize all of those quarterly job performance reviews you had prior to and during the merger with the new management.			
8. Create and enhance your network within the new company. List what you have done in this area.			

Activities	Response	Date	Comments
9. At the beginning of this phase, list aspects of the new culture and ways of doing things.			
10. Make yourself available in the development of SOPs and WPs in the new company, and influence the way in which they are developed.			
11. Last not but least, verify and check your various financial packages within the company.			

Bonus Chapter: Career- Building Checklist

Successful professional careers are built by careful planning from the very beginning, developing good work habits, developing short-term and long-term strategies, sheer hard work, and, to some extent, luck. Career building, in some aspects, is akin to *Wheel of Fortune*; it has a luck component and also has a strategy of jeopardy component. One technique that may help you to be successful is to look at the final career you would like to have and plan backward and plan accordingly. As an example, suppose that you are an entry-level engineer in a Fortune 100 company, and you wish to target the job of chief technology officer (CTO) or chief executive officer (CEO) of the company. Now that you have identified the end product—you want to reach the CTO or CEO position—the following strategic planning could be considered:

1. Find out what job-related educational background is typically required for attaining the level. For example, if one needs a MBA degree with finance, figure out how you could achieve the degree. It could be that you earn the degree part time while working, or alternatively, you could quit the job and earn the degree full time.

You may want to do this after working for a period of three or four years.

2. Find out what type of experience is typically required for attaining the level and plan out how to get that experience. Higher-level jobs typically require varied experience. For example, research and development may require experience in technology transfer, production and quality control, commercial development, marketing, finance, and so forth. In most cases, it may not be feasible to acquire this type of varied experience. One can, however, get the varied experience by participating in several teams.

3. Build your interpersonal skills early in your career; this is the most critical skill you will need as you move up. Remember that you will be working with people above you, below you, and with you. Take some excellent courses in the area of team building.

4. To move up in an organization, one needs to be a qualitative leader, an out-of-the-box thinker, a motivator, a delegator, and the most-importantly- a- hard- worker.

5. Find a couple of mentors within the company. It is very important to have mentor in order to move up in the organization.

6. Always be a solution provider instead of a problem/issue identifier. Organizations, small or big, need leaders who provide effective solutions to issues.

7. Be an excellent verbal and written communicator. Communication is vital for moving ahead in the organization. E-mails are a blessing; however, they can create problems if they are not properly handled. In any kind of communication, be courteous, firm, clear, and concise. Never use rough language—it seldom helps careers.

8. Always take care of the associates who report to you. Remember that people who report to you are your jewels and assets. Nurture them and help them grow. It is good for both you and them. Sometimes you may come across an associate who may not support you and may even work against you. Try to win them as much as you can, and if it does not work, try to push them out to another department.

9. If you are an entry-level employee, learn from your superior about what to do to move up in the ranks. You can learn what to do and what not to do.

10. Keep track of your career advancement by regularly checking where you are in comparison with your goals. If there are significant gaps, find ways to fill up the gaps by having development plans. Make appropriate adjustments, such as taking additional courses and training, changing departments, or even changing jobs.

11. Always participate in professional organizations by volunteering in various activities such as speaking. By engaging in professional organizations, you will come to know others in your profession, and others will come to know you, resulting in networking. This networking will be beneficial in the short term as well as long term.

12. In order to grow in any organization, one needs self-esteem, self-confidence, and a positive attitude. Recognizing that these three characteristics are of the utmost importance, one should keep a fine balance between self-confidence and arrogance. Don't become arrogant; that will hurt your career.

About the Author

The author is a survivor of seven mergers and acquisitions and several reorganizations in his career. This book is a summary of his extensive experience in the healthcare industry. The discussion provided in the book directly comes from his dealings during merger and acquisition or reorganization changes he went through in his professional career. The author is a consultant in the healthcare industry.